CONTENTS :: BOOK 3

D0333854

Enter

INTRODUCTION

Remember!

Remember!

This book will take your programming skills to the next level. We'll start off by working with the easy-to-use programming language Scratch. Then we will move on to a more complex language called Python. You are going to learn concepts including selection, how to use 'if' statements, and how to work with random numbers.

Refresh your memory

In Book 2, we learnt how to work with Scratch and how to use loops and variables. In case you've forgotten, here's a quick refresher on all that.

Let's remind ourselves how Scratch works. You can make a sprite move around the 'stage' area in the top left of the screen. Commands are in the form of blocks, which you join together to make programs.

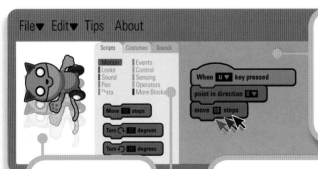

This is the scripts area – drag your command blocks over here. If you need to remove a command, drag it off the scripts area.

This area is called the stage.

Choose the group of commands from here.

Loops can be used to repeat commands. Both of these pieces of code draw a square.

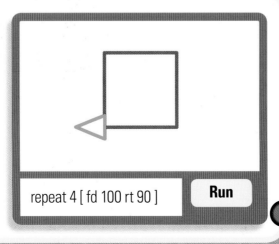

```
repeat 4 [ fd 100 rt 90 ]          Run
```

Variables can be used to store information.

Age = 8

AGE

4

HOW TO CODE

A STEP-BY-STEP GUIDE TO COMPUTER CODING

1 2 **3** 4

Book 3

Max Wainewright

INFORMATION ON RESOURCES

Here's how you can get hold of Scratch and Python so you can start experimenting.

SCRATCH

You can use Scratch on a PC or Mac by opening your web browser and going to: **http://scratch.mit.edu** – then click **'Create'** or **'Try it out'**.

There is a very similar website called Snap that also works on iPads. It is available here: **http://snap.berkeley.edu/run**

If you want to run Scratch without using the internet, you can download it from here:
http://scratch.mit.edu/scratch2download/

INSTALLING PYTHON ON A PC

1. Go to: **www.python.org**.
2. Click **'Downloads'** then choose **'Download Python'** (version 3.4 or higher).
3. Double-click the downloaded file, then follow the instructions on screen.
4. Click the **'Start'** button, click **'Python'**, then click **'IDLE'**. (In Windows 8, go to the top right of the screen and click **'Search'**, then type in 'idle' and click the program to run it.)

INSTALLING PYTHON ON A MAC

1. Go to: **www.python.org**.
2. Click **'Downloads'** then choose **'Download Python'** (version 3.4 or higher).
3. Double-click the downloaded file, then follow the instructions on screen.
4. To start using Python quickly, click **'Spotlight'** (at the top right of the screen).
5. Type 'idle' **Spotlight** idle then press **'Enter'**.

Making an icon for Python on a Mac (this will make it easier to find):

1. Open **'Finder'**.
2. Under the **'Go'** menu, click on **'Applications'**.
3. Scroll down to **Python** and click on it.
4. Drag the **IDLE** icon to the 'dock' (menu bar) at the bottom or side of the screen.

Design and illustration: Mike Henson
Editor: Claudia Martin
Project Editor: Carly Madden
Consultant: Sean McManus
Editorial Director: Victoria Garrard
Art Director: Laura Roberts-Jensen

First published in the UK in 2015 by
QED Publishing
Part of The Quarto Group
The Old Brewery,
6 Blundell Street,
London, N7 9BH

www.qed-publishing.co.uk

A catalogue record for this book is available from the British Library.

ISBN 978 1 78493 238 1

Printed in China

Scratch is developed by the Lifelong Kindergarten Group at MIT Media Lab. See http://scratch.mit.edu

Python is copyright (c) 1990–2014 Python Software Foundation; All Rights Reserved. It is downloadable and freely usable under an open source license. Applications in Python can be redistributed without reference to the Python Software Foundation.

Internet safety

Children should be supervised when using the internet, particularly when using an unfamiliar website for the first time.
The publisher and author cannot be held responsible for the content of the websites referred to in this book.

Download our robots to use as sprites on Scratch! Go to http://www.qed-publishing.co.uk/extra-resources.php or scan this:

What you will learn

In the next few pages, you'll learn how to use 'if' statements to select different parts of a program.

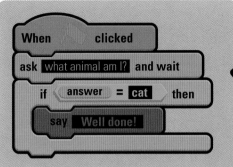

```
When        clicked
ask what animal am I? and wait
    if   answer  =  cat   then
        say  Well done!
```

Quiz Master

You'll learn how to write simple programs using a programming language called Python.

```
for n in range(1,101):
    print(n)
```

You will find out how to program with random numbers to make your own random pieces of art.

You'll even find out how to program a random sandwich using Python!

```
from random import *
f1=["cheese", "egg", "jam"]
f2=["carrot", "cress", "pickle"]
```

'IF' COMMANDS

I have made a plan of what we need to do.

Ask a question. If the answer is correct, say 'Well done'.

We need to use
if answer =

Ask 'What animal am I?' If answer = cat, say 'Well done'.

Quiz Master

Sometimes we want to run different bits of code in response to a question or input in a program. We can do this by using 'if' commands. This is called selection. Let's make a quiz to try it out.

Question time

1

Start Scratch (see page 2) and click **'Create'** or **'Try it out'**. Click the **'Scripts'** tab in the centre of the Scratch screen. Select the **Events** group.

Drag a **'When green flag clicked'** code block to the scripts area.

> Events
> Control
> Sensing
> **when** / **clicked**

Download our robots to use as sprites on Scratch! Go to http://www.qed-publishing.co.uk/extra-resources.php or scan here:

Key word

Selection: The way a computer program chooses which commands to run, after a simple question or value check.

What animal am I?

Click the green flag icon to test your code.

2

Click the **Sensing** group.

Drag an **'Ask and wait'** code block to join it.

Change the question text to 'What animal am I?'

> ~~Events~~
> Control
> Sensing
> Operators
> More Blocks
>
> **when** / **clicked**
> **ask** What animal am I? **and wait**

cat ✓

3

Now we need our program to check if the answer is correct. Click the **Control** group.

Drag an '**If then**' code block to join your program.

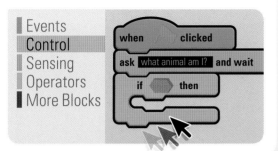

4

Click the **Operators** group.

Drag a green '**Equals**' box onto the '**If then**' block.

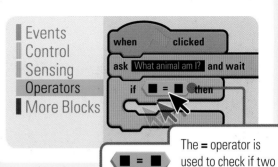

The **=** operator is used to check if two values are the same.

5

Click the **Sensing** group.

Drag an '**Answer**' code block into the left square in the '**Equals**' block.

Now click inside the right-hand square in the '**Equals**' block and type in the correct answer: cat.

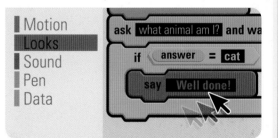

6

Click the **Looks** group.

Drag a '**Say Hello!**' code block into the middle of the '**If then**' block.

Change the text to say 'Well done!'.

Click the green flag icon to test your code.

Saving your work

Click the '**File**' menu at the top of the page on the left. Then click:
Download to your computer – to save a file onto your computer.
Upload from your computer – to open a file you saved earlier.
New – to start some new work.

Challenge

Can you think of a more difficult question?

Quiz Master

QUIZ TIME

To make a better quiz, we need to find a way to ask several questions. We also need to keep a score of our right answers. To do this, we can add a score variable.

Capital quiz

1

Start Scratch.

Build a quiz with one question. Turn back to the previous page if you need help.

Change the question and answer text.

Test your code.

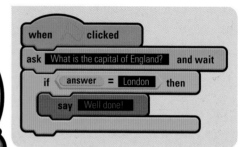

2

We need to make the program wait before asking the next question.

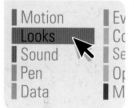

Click the **Looks** group.

Remove the **'Say Well Done!'** code block.

Replace it with a **'Say Hello! for 2 secs'** block. Change the text to 'Well done!'

3

Click the **Sensing** group.

Drag an **'Ask and wait'** code block to join after the **'If then'** block.

Type in the next question.

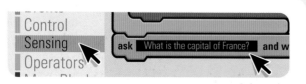

4

Drag in code to check the answer to your second question. Turn back to the previous page if you need help.

Test your code.

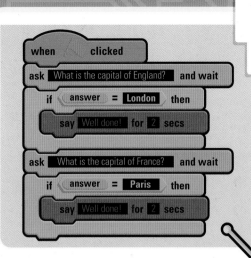

Your program should look like this.

Key word

Variable: A value stored by a computer program.

5

Now make a variable to keep the score.

OK

Then click **'OK'**.

Click the **Data** group.

Click **'Make a variable'**.

Call your variable 's' for score.

Test your code. Watch the score go up at the top left of the stage area.

6

To reset the score to 0 at the start of the quiz, drag a **'Set s to 0'** code block from the **Data** group here.

To make the score go up when question 1 is answered correctly, drag a **'Change s by 1'** code block here.

Put another one here for this question.

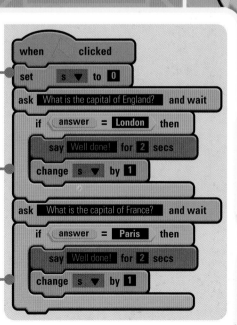

Challenge

Can you add some more questions?

Change the code to give 2 points for each correct answer.

9

'ELSE' COMMANDS

Key word

Operator: A piece of code that carries out a mathematical or logical operation.

We've learnt how to use selection to check if something is true. What about if it is false – if someone gives the wrong answer to a question? We can use 'else' commands to run a different bit of code in this case.

Wrong answer

1

Start Scratch.

Make one question. Turn to page 6 for help if you need it.

Change the question text.

```
when   clicked
ask   What is 10 + 10?   and wait
```

2

Click the **Control** group.

Drag an **'If then else'** code block to join your program.

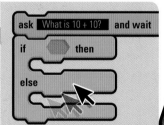

```
Events
Control
Sensing
Operators
More Blocks
```
```
ask   What is 10 + 10?   and wait
if          then

else

```

3

Drag in code to check the answer to the question.

If you need help, turn back to page 7.

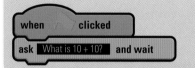

```
ask   What is 10 + 10?   and wait
if    answer  =  20   then
```

4

Now we need to make the program give a message to the player, depending on their answer.

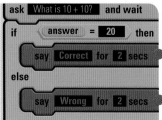

```
Motion
Looks
Sound
Pen
Data
```
```
ask   What is 10 + 10?   and wait
if    answer  =  20   then
    say  Correct  for  2  secs
else
    say  Wrong  for  2  secs
```

Drag a **'Say for 2 secs'** code block into the top gap and type in 'Correct'.

Drag a **'Say for 2 secs'** code block into the bottom gap and type in 'Wrong'.

Now try adding another question to your quiz. Use another **'If then else'** code block so the player gets told if each answer is right or wrong.

Higher or lower?

We know how to check if an answer, or variable, is equal to a value. Now we will learn to use 'Less than' or 'More than' operators to compare how big a variable is. We are going to make a small program that checks how old the player is before it starts.

1

Start a new program.

File ▼ Edit ▼
New

Make code to ask 'How old are you?'

when clicked
ask How old are you? and wait

2

From the **Control** group, drag an **'If then else'** code block to join your program.

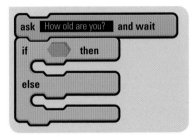

Click the **Operators** group.

Drag a **'Less than'** code block onto the **'If then else'** block.

Sensing
Operators
More Blocks

ask How old are you? and
if ■ < ■ then

3

Click the **Sensing** group. Drag an **'Answer'** code block into the left square in the **'Less than'** block. Type '8' into the right square.

answer < 8

4

Click the **Looks** group.

Motion
Looks
Sound
Pen
Data

ask How old are you? and wait
if answer < 8 then
say You are too young! for 2 secs
else
say Enjoy the game. for 2 secs

Drag a **'Say for 2 secs'** code block into the top gap and type in a message.

Drag a **'Say for 2 secs'** code block into the bottom gap and type in a message.

You can add a 'Stop' command after the 'Say' command to stop the program.

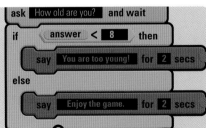

Stop all ▼

You can start the rest of your program below here. Only players aged 8 and over could use it.

Challenge

Try making the 'How old are you?' program using the 'More than' operator instead of 'Less than'.

Selection can be really useful in games. For example, we can use 'If then' command blocks to check if one sprite has touched another.

Apple-eating game

We are going to make a game where a cat sprite has to eat four apples. We will have to make lots of apple sprites by duplicating them.

We need to plan this in three parts.

1.
Move the cat to follow the mouse cursor.

2.
If the cat has touched an apple, hide the apple and make the score go up.

3.
Make lots of apples!

1

First we will drag code to the scripts area to make the Scratch sprite move slowly across the screen, pointing towards the mouse pointer.

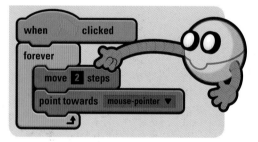

Drag the **'When green flag clicked'** code block from the **Events** group. Get the **'Forever'** loop block from the **Control** group, and the other blocks from the **Motion** group. Change the speed of the sprite to move 2 steps each loop.

Click the green flag icon near the top of the Scratch screen to test your code.

2

Click the **Data** group to make a variable called 's' for the score.

Look at step 5 on page 9 for help.

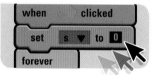

Drag a **'Set s to 0'** code block above the **'Forever'** loop.

3

Now add an apple sprite.

Click this icon.

Scroll down to the apple and click on it.

Then click **'OK'**.

I'm making an apple disappear!

4

Now we will drag code to the scripts area to control the apple.

Get the **'When green flag clicked'** code block from the **Events** group.

Get the **'Show'** code block from the **Looks** group and the **'Forever'** loop from the **Control** group.

The **'Show'** code block will make sure the apple is visible at the start of the game.

5

Every loop, we must check if the cat has touched the apple. If it has, the score must go up.

Join together these blocks of code.

You'll find the **'If then'** block in the **Control** group, the **'Touching'** block in the **Sensing** group, the **'Hide'** block in the **Looks** group, and the **'Change s by 1'** block in the **Data** group.

Set the **'Touching'** code block to 'Sprite1' – the cat.

6

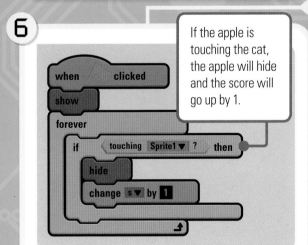

If the apple is touching the cat, the apple will hide and the score will go up by 1.

Drag the **'If then'** code block into the **'Forever'** loop.

This will mean the **'If touching'** check will run on every loop forever.

7

Finally, right-click the apple and click **'Duplicate'**. (If you're using a Mac, you'll need to hold the **'Control'** key and click.)

Drag the new apple to a space and then duplicate two more apples.

Test your game!

When the apples are duplicated, their code is duplicated too!

Challenge

Make your own game with different sprites. How about making the apples move when the flag is clicked?

STARTING PYTHON

Python is a computer language that will help you learn more complex ideas and techniques. In Scratch, we dragged commands around to make a program. With Python, you need to type all the commands very carefully to make your programs work.

Installing Python

Python is free to download, and comes with something called IDLE which lets you type and edit Python programs.

You need to download and install Python before you start coding. Ask an adult to help you. Check that they don't mind you installing some software on the computer. See page 2 for help.

Using Python

1 Start IDLE, the Python editor.

Woohoo... download!

ON A **WINDOWS** COMPUTER

Click   **'Start'**
       'Programs'
       'Python'
       'IDLE'

On Windows 8, go to top right of the screen:

Click **'Search'**
Type **'idle'**
Click on the program to run it

ON A **MAC**

Click **'Spotlight'** 🔍 (top right of the screen)

Type **'idle'**   Spotlight | idle

Press **'Enter'**

2 Click **'File'** then **'New file'**.

File   Edit
New File

3

The command **print** tells Python to display text on the screen. Type this code:

```
print ("hello")
```

Make sure you type commands in lower case, not capitals!

Your text will change colour automatically to show parts of the code. **Print** will be purple and **"hello"** will be green.

Make sure you type really carefully. You need both brackets and both quotes for your code to work.

4

You must save your code before you run it.

Click **'File'** then **'Save'** (to the desktop).

Name as **'test'** then press **'Enter'**.

5

Run your code!

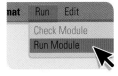

Click **'Run'** then **'Run module'**.

```
print ("hello")
```

```
>>>
hello
>>>
```

The output from your program will be shown in another window.

If it doesn't work, check your code carefully and try again.

Congratulations!
You have made your first Python program. Click **'File'** then **'Exit'** and practise steps 1 to 5 again.

Change your program to say something else, like...

'Goodbye!'

PYTHON PRINTING

Now we are going to write a few simple Python programs. To start off, we are going to practise using Python to print text on the screen. Then we'll get Python to do simple calculations and print the answer.

Hello!

Hello world!

1. Start IDLE, the Python editor. Turn back to page 14 for help if you need it.

2. Click **'File'** then **'New'**.

3. Type your code:
   print("hello")
   print("world")

   Press **'Enter'** after each line.

4. Click **'File'** then **'Save'**. Choose a file name and press **'Enter'**.

5. Click **'Run'**, then **'Run module'** to test your code. The output from your program should look like this:

   ```
   >>>
   hello
   world
   >>>
   ```

Making calculations

1. Click **'File'** then **'New'**.

2. Type your code:
   print("ten plus ten is")
   print(10 + 10)

   You don't need quotes when doing a calculation.

3. Save then run your code. (Look at steps 4 and 5 on the right.) The output should look like this:

   ```
   >>>
   ten plus ten is
   20
   >>>
   ```

This is how Python runs a program with several lines of code.

16

Do your sums

Now try typing in the following programs. Follow the usual steps to start a new program, save it and run it each time.

1

```
print("twenty plus twenty is")
print(20 + 20)
```

2

```
print("fifty plus twenty is")
print(50 + 20)
```

3

```
print("ten times ten is")
print(10 * 10)
```

4

```
print("four plus four is")
print(4 + 4)
print("eight times eight is")
print(8 * 8)
```

See page 30 for the answers.

Computer programs use **✳** instead of **x** to do multiplication.

Remember: you don't need quotes when doing calculations, but you do need brackets!

Shortcuts

A quick way to save your work is to hold down **'Control'** and press **S**. (On a Mac, hold ⌘ then press **S**.)

A shortcut to running your code is just pressing the **F5** key at the top of the keyboard.

Challenge

Write a program with your own sums and calculations in.

Use **-** to do subtraction and **/** to do division.

Can you make a program to work out the number of hours in a year?

PYTHON QUESTIONS

After working with Scratch, using Python can seem a bit more fiddly. However, there are some things that can be done very easily with Python. We're going to use inputs, variables and 'if' commands to code a simple quiz.

Is that you?

1. Start IDLE, the Python editor. Turn back to page 14 for help if you need it.
2. Click **'File'** then **'New'**.
3. We need to make Python ask a question. Type in this code:

```
name=input("what is your name? ")
```

4. Click **'File'** then **'Save'**. Choose a file name and press **'Enter'**.
5. Click **'Run'** then **'Run module'** to test your code. The output from your program should look like this:

```
>>>
what is your name?
>>>
```

Type your answer here and press **'Enter'**.

What is your name?

Errr...

The first line of code tells Python to store what the user types in a variable called 'name'.

The second line tells it to print 'hello' and whatever it stored.

6. We want Python to say 'hello' to the user. Add a second line to your code:

```
name=input("what is your name?")
print("hello", name)
```

Save and run your code. What do you think will happen?

7 We can change our code so it only says 'hello' if your name is Max.

```
name=input("what is your name?")
if name=="Max":
    print("Hello coder!")
```

Type in this code.

IDLE should put in a tab here for you. If not, press the **'Tab'** key yourself!

...errr...

Max?!?

Key word

Input: An action (like typing in an answer) that tells a program to do something.

8 Save and run your code to test it. Try changing the name you type.

Hello coder!

Make sure you type everything very carefully:

Two equals signs

Colon
:

```
if name=="Max":
    print("Hello coder!")
```

Tab

The 'if' command checks if something is true. The next line only runs if it is true.

Quiz time

Now you know enough to code your own quiz. Start with the question shown here: 'What is the capital of England?' Then, try adding some more questions of your own.

```
a=input("what is the capital of England?")
if a=="London":
    print("Correct")
```

```
>>>
what is the capital of England? London
Correct
>>>
```

PYTHON LOOPS

We've already looked at how we can print things on the screen with Python. Now we are going to learn how to use loops in Python that will allow us to print things over and over again.

Why use loops?

1. Start up Python (see page 14).

2. Type in the following program:

```
print(1)
print(2)
print(3)
print(4)
print(5)
```

3. Save and run the program. You should see the numbers 1 to 5 printed on the screen.

```
>>>
1
2
3
4
5
>>>
```

If we wanted to count up to 10, we could add more print commands. But if we wanted to count up to 100, it would take a very long time to program. It would also mean we had to change the program every time we wanted to count to a different number.

Instead we can create a loop to count up to any number very easily. We need to use the 'for' command:

Variable (called **n**) to do the counting. You could call it any letter you like.

Starting number

Number above the highest number we want to count to

Don't forget the colon.

```
for n in range(1,11):
    print(n)
```

IDLE should put in a tab here for you. If not, press the **'Tab'** key yourself!

Put any commands you want to be repeated here. In this case, it's the commands to print out the numbers 1–10.

Key word

Loop: A series of commands repeated a number of times.

Counting to 100

① Start up Python and type in the following program:

```
for n in range(1,101):
    print(n)
```

② Save and run the program.

You should see the numbers 1 to 100 whizz by on the screen.

```
>>>
1
2
…
98
99
100
>>>
```

print ("DANGER!")
print ("DANGER!")

print ("number stampede!")

Have a go

Type in these programs. Before you run them, try to predict what they will do. Check your answers on page 30.

①
```
for n in range(1,21):
    print(n)
```

②
```
for n in range(1,51):
    print(n)
```

③
```
for a in range(1,201):
    print(a)
```

④
```
for b in range(1,101):
    print(b*10)
```

⑤
```
for c in range(1,101):
    print(c*100)
```

Remember * means multiply.

PYTHON GRAPHICS

We can draw graphics – such as diagrams and pictures – in Python by borrowing a special group of commands called a library. We need to tell Python we are going to use the library at the start of our program. We can then use commands in a similar way to how we directed the turtle or sprite in Logo and Scratch (Book 1).

Turtle time

A turtle is a robot, sprite or arrow that can be given commands to move around. In Python, the library of commands that allows us to draw pictures is called the 'turtle library'. It tells the turtle – an arrow – how to move and draw. We are going to learn how to use it.

1. Start up Python.
2. Type in the following program:

```
from turtle import *
forward(200)
```

This tells Python to borrow all the commands from the turtle library and bring them into our program.

3. Save and run the program. A new window will open to show the turtle graphics. The **forward(200)** command will draw a line like this:

4. We can make the turtle turn left and right by using commands called **left** and **right**! Try adding these commands to your program:

```
from turtle import *
forward(200)
right(90)
forward(200)
right(90)
```

This tells the turtle to make a right turn of 90 degrees – a right angle.

Make sure there isn't a space at the start of a line.

Save and run the program.

Now try this

Try these exercises. Check your answers on page 30!

1. Add more code to finish drawing a square.
2. Try changing your code to draw a rectangle.

Don't forget to type **from turtle import *** at the start of your program.

Loops and graphics

On page 20, we found out how loops can repeat commands when counting. We can use the same idea to draw shapes. We will use a variable called **n** to count the number of times to repeat the loop. Type in this code:

```
from turtle import *
for n in range(0,4):
    forward(200)
    right(90)
```

This loop draws four sides of a square. We could pick any letter as a counting variable. We have used **n**.

The colon will add a tab to the start of the next line.

Key word

Library: A collection of commands that are already stored and ready for use.

Then try this

Now type the following programs. Predict which of these shapes each one will draw before saving and running it. The answers are on page 30.

1
```
from turtle import *
for n in range(0,6):
    forward(200)
    right(60)
```

2
```
from turtle import *
for n in range(0,8):
    forward(100)
    right(45)
```

3
```
from turtle import *
for n in range(0,5):
    forward(200)
    right(72)
```

4
```
from turtle import *
for n in range(0,5):
    forward(200)
    right(144)
```

RANDOM PYTHON

It would be dull if games were always the same each time we played them. With a board game, we can throw a dice to choose how far a player moves each time. In a computer game, we can get the computer to pick a random number.

randint(1,6)

Randint means 'random integer' (a random whole number).

Between 1 and 6

Random number

1. Start up Python and type in the below command. **Random** tells Python that we are going to use random numbers. **Import** tells Python to borrow commands from a library to do this.

```
from random import *
```

2. Now print a random number:

```
from random import *
print(randint(1,6))
```

3. Save and run the program. A number between 1 and 6 will be shown. Each time you run the program, a new number will be picked. For example:

Heads or tails?

We can also mimic tossing a coin. We are going to use a command called **choice**, which will pick a word from a list.

1. Start a new Python program. Type in:

This makes a list of two words called 'coin'. Make sure you type the double quotes and square brackets carefully.

```
from random import *
coin=["heads", "tails"]
print(choice(coin))
```

This tells Python to pick a word randomly from the list called 'coin'.

2. Save and run the program. The program will print 'heads' or 'tails'. Run the program again to test it.

Make a sandwich

Finally we are going to teach Python how to make a sandwich. We are going to make two lists of fillings and randomly pick one from each.

1 Click **'File'** and **'New file'** to start a new Python program.

2 Type in:

```
from random import *
f1=["cheese", "egg", "jam"]
f2=["carrot", "cress", "pickle"]
```

3 Add a final line:

```
print(choice(f1), "and", choice(f2))
```

4 Save and run the program to see a random sandwich!

```
>>>
jam and pickle
>>>
```

```
>>>
cheese and cress
>>>
```

5 Now you could change your code to make 10 sandwiches at once, using a 'for' loop:

```
from random import *
f1=["cheese", "egg", "jam"]
f2=["carrot", "cress", "pickle"]
for s in range(0,10):
    print(choice(f1),"and", choice(f2), "sandwich")
```

Key word

Import: To take data from one program into another.

Here is a list of my favourite fillings. Don't forget the commas and double quotes. Add a square bracket at each end.

My list is called f2.

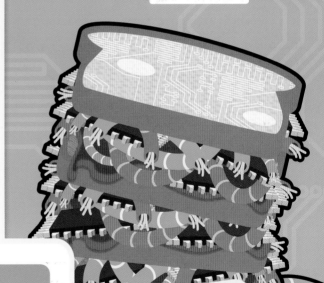

Challenge

Add a third filling by making another list called f3.

RANDOM ART

Let's turn back to Scratch to see how we can use random numbers to control computer graphics. By picking random numbers for the place we draw a circle, how big and what colour it is, we can make a random piece of art.

Coordinates

We choose where to draw by setting the x and y coordinates of the sprite:

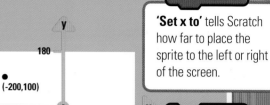

'Set x to' tells Scratch how far to place the sprite to the left or right of the screen.

'Set y to' tells Scratch how far to place the sprite up or down the screen.

Random bubble art

①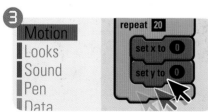

Start Scratch. See page 2 for help. Click the **Pen** group. Drag a **'Clear'** and a **'Pen down'** code block to the scripts area.

②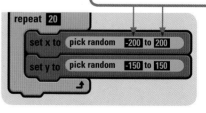

Click the **Control** group. Drag a **'Repeat'** code block beneath them. Change it to make 20 loops.

Change the range of the random numbers.

③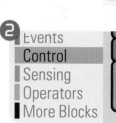

Click the **Motion** group. Drag a **'Set x to'** and a **'Set y to'** code block into the 'Repeat' loop.

④

To make the lines random, click the **Operators** group. Drag a **'Pick random'** code block into the circle of the **'Set x to'** code block. Do the same for the **'Set y to'** block.

5

Click any block in the code to test your program.

Your art should look a bit like this.

6

Now we will draw random blobs.

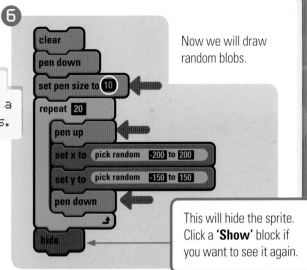

This will hide the sprite. Click a **'Show'** block if you want to see it again.

Click the **Pen** group. Drag **'Set pen size to'**, **'Pen up'** and **'Pen down'** code blocks into your program. Change the pen size to 10. From the **Looks** group, drag a **'Hide'** code block to the end of your program.

Changing the pen size will draw more thickly. **'Pen up'** and **'Pen down'** will draw blobs rather than lines.

Click the first command to test your program.

7

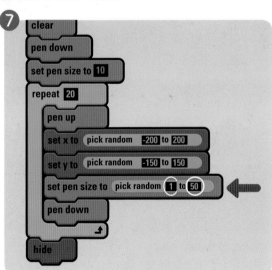

You can change the size of the blobs by adding another **'Set pen size'** and a **'Pick random'** code block (from the **Operators** group). Change the range of random numbers to choose the smallest and biggest blob size. Test it!

8

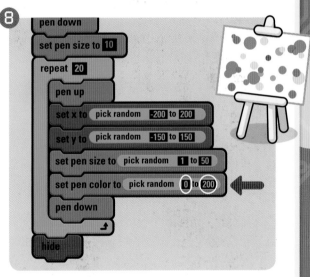

Finally add a **'Set pen color to 0'** (note the American spelling of 'colour') from the **Pen** group and a **'Pick random'** code block (from the **Operators** group) in to your program. Choose the range of colours you want. Test your program. Now experiment with all the random number ranges and how many times the loop runs.

DEBUGGING

Coding can be a process of trial and error – testing ideas and seeing if they work. It is normal to make mistakes when coding. A bug is another name for a mistake in a piece of code that stops it working properly. Debugging means fixing those mistakes. Try these exercises then check your answers on page 31.

1

This Scratch program should only say 'Well done' when the answer is 4. But it says 'Well done' all the time. Debug it!

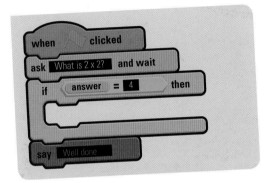

2

This program should only say 'Well done' when the answer is 25. But it says 'Well done' except when the answer is 25. What's gone wrong?

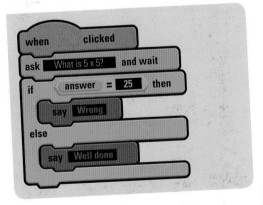

3

This code is part of a game where a dog has to catch a cat. The player should get one point when it does – but the score goes back to 0 instead. Fix the code.

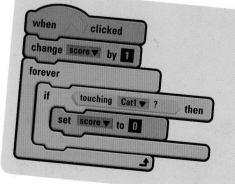

28

Python debugging

4

There are some small errors in each of these lines of Python code, so nothing is being shown. Debug each line.

a

```
prinnt("Hello everyone!")
```

b

```
Print("This is my program.")
```

c

```
print("Goodbye - hope you enjoyed it!)
```

5

This code should print the numbers from 1 to 10, but it stops at 9. Debug it!

```
for n in range(1,10):
    print(n)
```

6

Nothing happens with this code. It should print the numbers from 1 to 20. What's wrong?

```
for n in range(1,21):
print(n)
```

7

This code should print a random number between 1 and 6, but instead it always prints a 6. Debug it!

```
from random import *
print(randint(6,6))
```

Debugging guidelines

When your code doesn't do what you want it to:

1. Work through your code step by step, thinking about what each command does.
2. Draw a picture or diagram to help.
3. Have a break for a few minutes!

Think about these guidelines when you are coding:

1. Plan your program carefully – either with a diagram or some notes.
2. When you are learning to code, it is better to write lots of small, simple programs rather than one larger and more complex program.
3. Test your program as you build it. Don't wait until you have put in all the commands.

ANSWERS

Page 17

1
```
>>>
twenty plus twenty is
40
>>>
```

2
```
>>>
fifty plus twenty is
70
>>>
```

3
```
>>>
ten times ten is
100
>>>
```

4
```
>>>
four plus four is
8
eight times eight is
64
>>>
```

Page 21

1 1 2 3... 19 20

2 1 2 3... 49 50

3 1 2 3... 199 200

4 10 20 30... 990 1000

5 100 200 300... 9900 10000

Page 22

1
```
from turtle import *
forward(200)
right(90)
forward(200)
right(90)
forward(200)
right(90)
forward(200)
right(90)
```

2
```
from turtle import *
forward(200)
right(90)
forward(100)
right(90)
forward(200)
right(90)
forward(100)
right(90)
```

Page 23

1 Hexagon

2 Octagon

3 Pentagon

4 Star

1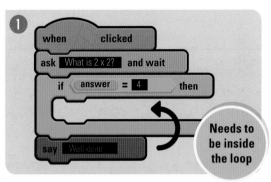

Needs to be inside the loop

2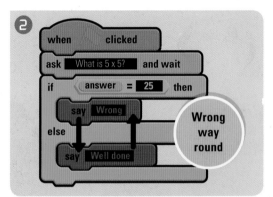

Wrong way round

3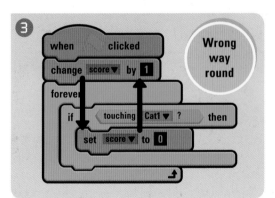

Wrong way round

4 a) **prinnt** should be **print** (only 1 n)
b) **Print** should be **print** (not capital P)
c) **it!)** should be **it!")** (missing quote at end)

5 **range(1,11)** not **(1,10)**

6 **print(n)** should start with a tab:
.... **print(n)**

7 **randint(1,6)** not **(6,6)**

Other books in the *How to Code* series:

BOOK 1

Introduction to the basic principles of coding. Experiment with Logo and Scratch. Move turtles and sprites across the screen!
ISBN: 978 1 78493 236 7

BOOK 2

Builds on basic coding and introduces loops and repetition. Code a maze game in Scratch or learn how to add sound effects!
ISBN: 978 1 78493 237 4

BOOK 4

Develop your coding techniques further by learning how to create web pages using HTML. Discover how to program in JavaScript. Build a website about pets!
ISBN: 978 1 78493 239 8

HOW TO CODE – THE GROWN-UPS' GUIDE

A handbook for parents and teachers, which provides background information and detailed explanations on all topics covered in Books 1–4.
ISBN: 978 1 78493 240 4

GLOSSARY

Code A set of special words or commands that tells a computer what to do.

Command A word or code block that tells the computer what to do.

Coordinates A set of numbers that gives the position of a point. It is common to use two numbers, called x and y. X gives the distance to the right or left of the screen. Y gives the distance up or down.

Data Information that can be stored and used by a computer.

Debugging Fixing problems (bugs) in a computer program.

Degree The unit of measurement for angles. If we turn all the way around, we turn 360 degrees. A quarter-turn is 90 degrees.

Download To copy data from one computer system to another using the internet.

Editor A program used to type and edit programs.

Graphics Data that is displayed as a picture, diagram or graph.

IDLE The editor used to write Python code.

If...then...else A common form of selection in coding, where a command is run if something is true, and a different command is run if it is false.

Import To take data from one program into another.

Input An action (such as pressing a key) that tells a program to do something.

Integer A whole number, such as 1 or 24.

Language A system of words, numbers, symbols and rules for writing programs.

Library A collection of commands that are already stored and ready for use.

Logo A computer language in which commands move a turtle around the screen to draw.

Loop A sequence of commands repeated a number of times.

Operator A piece of code that carries out a mathematical or logical operation.

Output Something that a computer program does to show the results of a program, such as moving a sprite or making a sound.

Program The special commands that tell a computer how to do something.

Python A programming language that uses text (words, letters, numbers and keyboard symbols) to make a program.

Random When all possible choices have an equal chance of being picked.

Scratch A computer language that uses blocks to make a program.

Scripts area In Scratch, this is the area to the right of the Scratch screen, where you need to drag your code blocks to.

Selection The way a computer program chooses which commands to run, after a simple question or value check.

Sprite An object moving around the screen.

Stage In Scratch, this is the area to the top left of the Scratch screen, where you can watch your sprites move about.

Turtle A robot, sprite or arrow that can be programmed to move around the floor or computer screen.

Variable A value or piece of data stored by a computer program.

INDEX